HARDPRESS.NET

ISBN: 9781290551571

Published by:
HardPress Publishing
8345 NW 66TH ST #2561
MIAMI FL 33166-2626

Email: info@hardpress.net
Web: http://www.hardpress.net

MORE GOOPS

AND

HOW NOT TO BE THEM

MORE GOOPS

AND

HOW NOT TO BE THEM

A Manual of Manners for Impolite Infants
Depicting the Characteristics of Many
Naughty and Thoughtless Children
With Instructive Illustrations

By GELETT BURGESS

NEW YORK
Frederick A. Stokes Company
Publishers

TWELFTH PRINTING

Printed in the United States of America

CONTENTS

TABLE OF CONTENTS

INTRODUCTION

Children, although you might expect
My manners to be quite correct
(For since I fancy I can teach,
I ought to practice what I preach),
'T is true that I have often braved
My mother's wrath, and misbehaved!
And almost every single rule
I broke, before I went to school!
For that is how I learned the way
To teach you etiquette to-day.
So when you chance to take a look
At all the maxims in the book,
You 'll see that most of them are true,
I found them out, and so will you,
For if you are as GOOP derided,
You may perhaps reform, as I did!

WINDOW–SMOOCHERS

Little Goops are marking
  On the window pane;
  I forbid, in vain!
Noses, when they 're greasy,
Leave a smooch so easy!
  Rub it out again!
I shall have to scold them,
For I 've often told them,
  Kindly, to refrain!

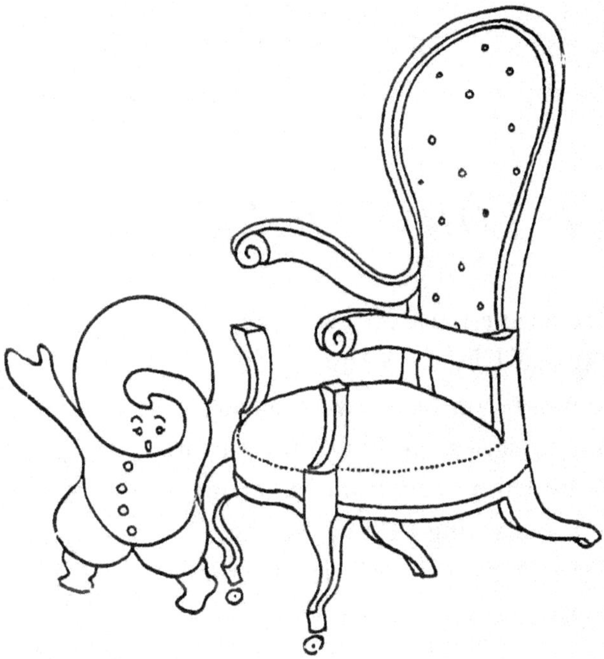

A LOW TRICK

THE meanest trick I ever knew
Was one I know *you* never do.
I saw a Goop once try to do it,
And there was nothing funny to it.
He pulled a chair from under me
As I was sitting down; but he
Was sent to bed, and rightly, too.
It was a *horrid* thing to do!

WHEN TO GO

WHEN you go a-calling,
  Never stay too late;
You will wear your welcome out
  If you hesitate!
Just before they're tired of you,
  Just before they yawn,
Before they think you are a Goop,
  And wish that you were gone,
While they're laughing with you,
  While they like you so,
While they want to keep you,—
  That's the time to go!

GRAMMAR

"AIN'T"

Now "ain't" is a word
That is very absurd
  To use for an "is n't" or "are n't."
Ask Teacher about it:
She'll say, "Do without it!"
  I wish you would see if you can't!

~~Ain't~~
Isn't
Arent

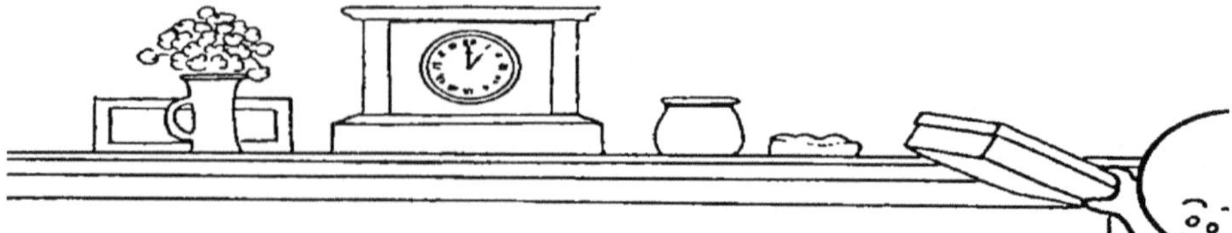

ELL THE NIBBLER

SHE ate some chocolate drops at 1,
  At 2, she thought she 'd take
A little jelly and a bun;
  At 3, some frosted cake.

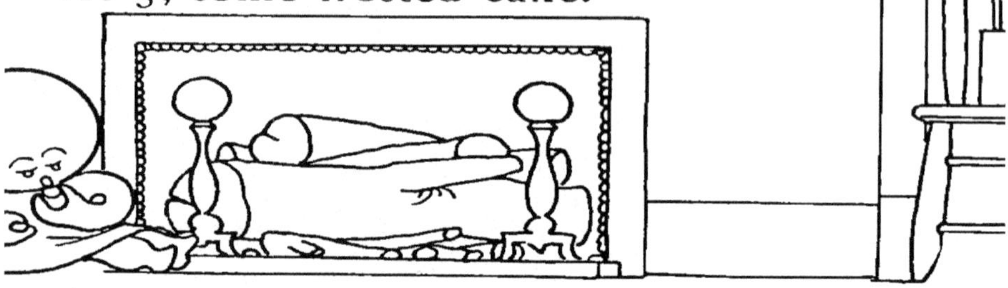

At 4, she nibbled at a roll;
  At 5, a doughnut spied,
And ate it (all except the hole),
  And then some cookies tried.

At 6, she did n't feel quite right,
  And did n't care for dinner.
She said she had no appetite,
  With so much Goop-food in her!

JUSTICE

WHENEVER brother 's sent to bed,
Or punished, do not go
And peer at him and jeer at him,
And say, "I told you so!"

Nor should you try to make him laugh
When he has been so bad;
Let him confess his naughtiness
Before you both are glad!

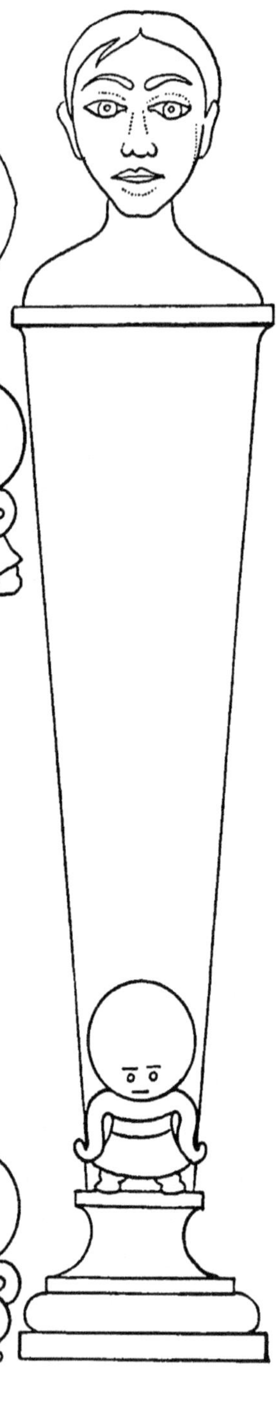

FRANKNESS

When you are talking, I expect
You'd better hold your head erect!
Please look me squarely in the eye
Unless you're telling me a lie.
For if you crouch and look askance,
Regarding me with sidelong glance,
I'll think it is a Goop I see
Who is *afraid* to look at me!

THE DUTY OF THE STRONG

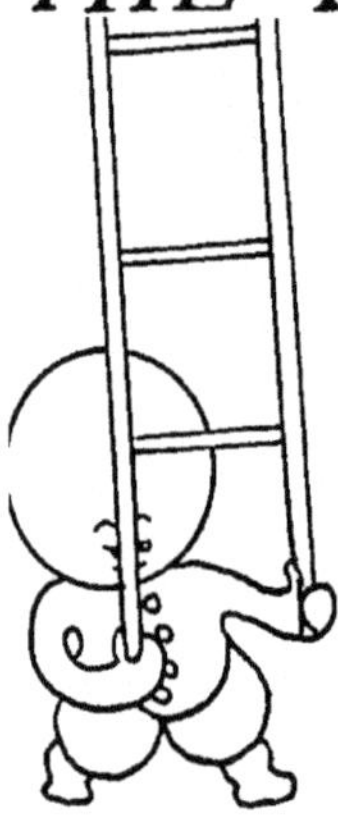

You who are the oldest,
You who are the tallest,
Don't you think you ought to help
The youngest and the smallest?

You who are the strongest,
You who are the quickest,
Don't you think you ought to help
The weakest and the sickest?

Never mind the trouble,
Help them all you can;
Be a little woman!
Be a little man!

WALKING WITH PAPA

"Won't you walk a little farther?"
  Said a Goop to his Papa;
"It is really quite delightful,
  And we haven't travelled far;
Won't you walk a little farther,
  There's a house I'd like to see!
Won't you walk a little farther,
  Till we reach that cherry-tree?"

"Won't you carry me? I'm tired!"
  Whined a Goop to his Papa;
"And my feet are sore and weary,
  And we've gone so *very* far!
Won't you carry me? I'm tired!
  And I *can't* walk back alone!
Won't you carry me? I'm tired!"
  And the Goop began to groan.

PIANO TORTURE

Pianos are considered toys
By Goops, and naughty girls and boys;
  They pound upon the keys,
They lift the cover up, on top,
To see the little jiggers hop,
  And both the pedals squeeze!

But instruments so rich and fine
(Especially if they're not mine)
  I ought to treat with care;
So when my elder sister plays
She'll find it is in tune always,
  Nor injured anywhere!

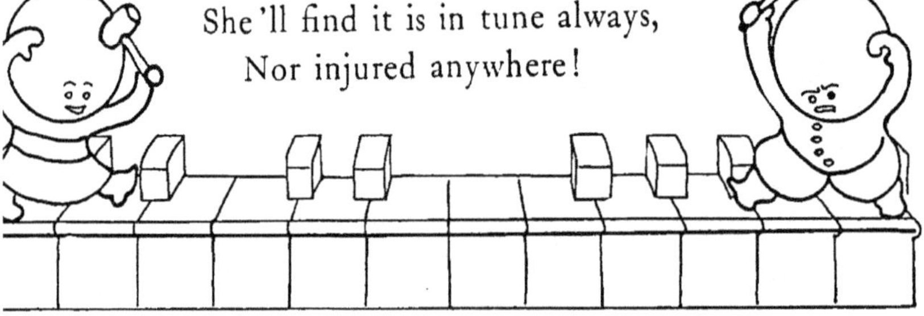

AT TABLE

Why is it Goops must always wish
To touch *each* apple on the dish?
Why do they never neatly fold
Their napkins until they are told?
Why do they play with food, and bite
Such awful mouthfuls? Is it right?
Why do they tilt back in their chairs?
Because they're Goops! So no one cares!

HOW TO EAT SOUP

Whenever you are eating soup
Remember not to be a Goop!
And if you think to say this rhyme,
Perhaps 'twill help you every time:

Like little boats that put to sea,
I push my spoon AWAY from me;
I do not tilt my dish, nor scrape
The last few drops, like hungry ape!

Like little boats, that, almost filled,
Come back without their cargoes spilled,
My spoon sails gently to my lips,
Unloading from the SIDE, like ships.

NOTICE
DO NOT
WAKE UP
THIS SEED!

BABY'S APOLOGY

Dear little seed, queer little seed,
  Tucked into bed in the garden,
Why don't you grow? Why, don't you know
  Baby is asking your pardon?

Out, little seed! Sprout, little seed!
  Baby did wrong without knowing!
Hoping for you, groping for you,
  To see if you *really* were growing.

Break, little seed! Wake, little seed!
  Baby will watch and not harm you.
Everything's bright, everything's right,
  Nothing is here to alarm you.

Dress, little seed! Yes, little seed,
  Fold your green leaflets around you;
There, little seed! Fair little seed,
  Baby's *so* glad he has found you!

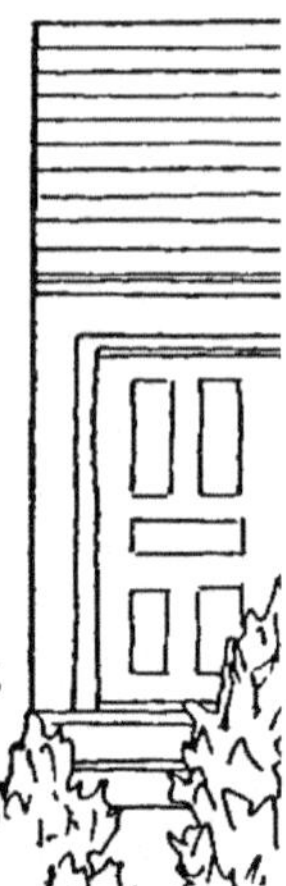

IN THE STREET

PEELINGS on the sidewalk,
  Apple-cores and all,
Kick them in the gutter;
  Save some one a fall!
Barrel hoops, glass, and cans,
  And wires in the street,
Kick them in the gutter;
  You'll save some horse's feet!

SICK FURNITURE

SITTING on the table,
Standing on the chairs,
That 's the way the legs are broken
and the cushion tears!
How 'd you like to pay the bill for varnish and repairs?

BORROWED PLUMES

Don't try on the wraps,
The bonnets and caps
Of company coming to call!
Admire, if you please,
But garments like these
Should always feel safe in the hall!

THE GOOP PICNIC

They came to the best sort of place for a rest,
On the grass, with the trees overhead,
They sat down in a bunch and they opened their lunch,
And they had a be-autiful spread!

And when they were done, and they 'd had all their fun,
They proved they were Goops, or were blind;
For they picked up their wraps and they left all their scraps
For the *next* picnic party to find!

WILD
BOOKS
I HAVE
MET
BY
A. GOOP

BOOK–MANNERS

If you scribble on your books,
How disgustable it looks!
Here a word, and there a scrawl,
Silly pictures over all!
Take a paper, or a slate,
If you want to decorate!

A.D.T.
MAY

POOR MOTHER!

Oh! Isn't it shocking!
Just look at your stocking!
Just look at your brand new boots!
Your waist is all torn
And your trousers are worn —
Just *look* at the holes in your suits!

Your father is working
All day, without shirking,
To pay for the clothes that you wear;
Your mother is mending
All day, and attending
To you, with the kindest of care.

And so, while you 're playing,
Think of father, who 's paying,
And mother, who 's working so hard;
While you kneel on your knees,
Or climb up the trees,
Or make your mud pies in the yard!

CHEATING

I THOUGHT I saw a little Goop
Who did n't pay his fare;
I looked again; the passengers
Were gazing at him, there.
"They think that he's a thief!" I said;
"I wonder does he care?"

GOOP! GOOP! GOOP!

Goop! Goop! Goop!
I wish you 'd wash your face!
Goop! Goop! Goop!
Your hands are a disgrace!
Goop! Goop! Goop!
Put things back in their place!
I wish you were polite,
Instead of a
Goop! Goop! Goop!

VISITING

WHEN a Goop goes out to visit,
'Tisn't very pleasant, is it,
To hear him ask his friends for things to eat?
And to hear the little sinner
Say he wants to stay to dinner
Is a piece of impoliteness hard to beat!
"*Mother said that I could stay*
"*If you asked me!*" is the way
That a Goop will make them ask him to remain.
It is better to be slighted
Than to stay when not invited,
For they *never* ask a Goop to come again!

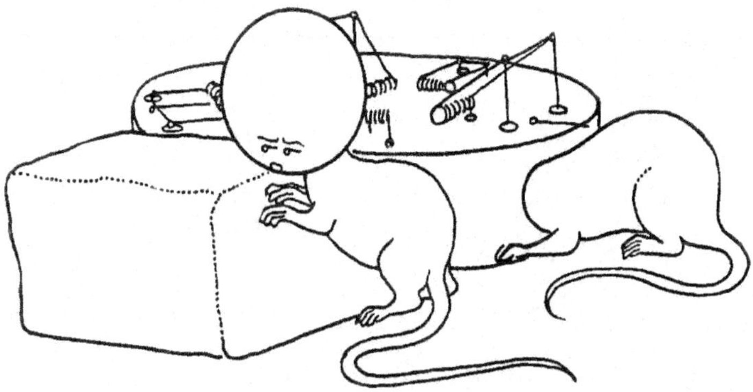

PICKING and STEALING

WHEN you are fetching bread, I trust
You never nibble at the crust.

When in the kitchen, do you linger
And pinch the cookies with your finger?

Or do you peck the frosted cake?
Don't do it, please, for Mother's sake!

LOYALTY

MOTHER's found your mischief out!
What are you going to do?
Cry and sulk, or kick and shout?
Tell your mother all about
Brother's mischief, too?

Or,
Take your punishment, and say,
"I'll be better, now!"
Never mind the horrid way
Brother treated you, at play;
Don't tell it, anyhow!

It is the Goops,
who have no shame,

Who say,

"'Twas some one else to blame!"

INDOLENCE

THERE was a Goop who lay in bed
Till half-past eight, the sleepy-head !
He could n't find his stockings, for
He 'd thrown them somewhere on the floor!
He could n't find his reading-book ;
He had forgotten where to look !
His breakfast grew so very cold,
This lazy Goop began to scold ;
And then he blamed his mother, kind !
" *You made me late to school !* "
he whined.

THE LAW OF HOSPITALITY

THERE is a very simple rule
   That every one should know;
You may not hear of it in school,
   But everywhere you go,
In every land where people dwell,
   And men are good and true,
You'll find they understand it well,
   And so I'll tell it you:

To every one who gives me food,
   Or shares his home with me,
I owe a debt of gratitude,
   And I must loyal be.
I may not laugh at him, or say
   Of him a word unkind;
His friendliness I must repay,
   And to his faults be blind!

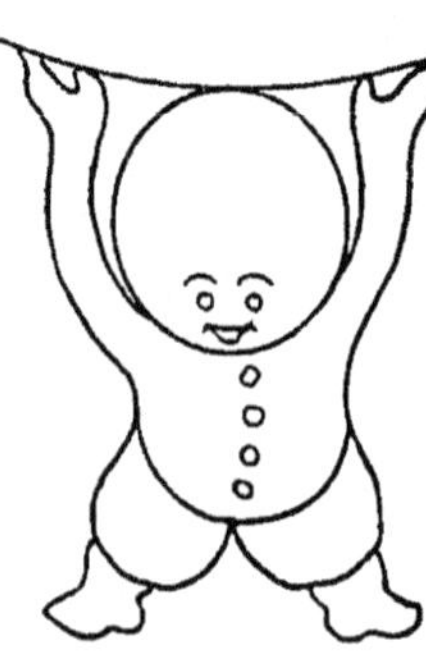

THE · FLOWER HOSPITAL

I DREAMED I found a sunlit room
Filled with a delicate perfume,
Where, moaning their sweet lives away,
A thousand lovely flowers lay.
They drooped, so pale, and wan, and weak,
With hardly strength enough to speak,
With stems so crushed and leaves so torn
It was too dreadful to be borne!
And one white lily raised her head
From off her snowy flower bed,
And sighed, "*Please tell the children, oh!*
They should not treat the flowers so!
They plucked us when we were so gay,
And then they threw us all away
To wither in the sun all day!
We all must fade, but we'll forgive
If they'll let other flowers live!"

PUPPY GOOPS

Candy in the cushions
   Of the easy-chair ;
Raisins in the sofa —
   How did they get there ?
The little Goop who 's greedy
   Does it every day,
Like a little puppy,
   Hiding bones away !

EXAGGERATION

DON'T try to tell a story
  To beat the one you 've heard;
For if you try, you 're apt to lie,
  And *that* would be absurd!

Don't try to be more funny
  Than any one in school;
For if you 're not, they 'll laugh a lot,
  And think you are a fool!

NOISE! NOISE! NOISE!

Do you slam the door?
   Do you drag your feet?
Making noise enough for four
Hundred thousand Goops, or more,
   Tearing up the street?

Clattering down the stairs,
   Storming through the hall,
Pounding floors, upsetting chairs,
Do you think your father cares
   For your noise, at all?

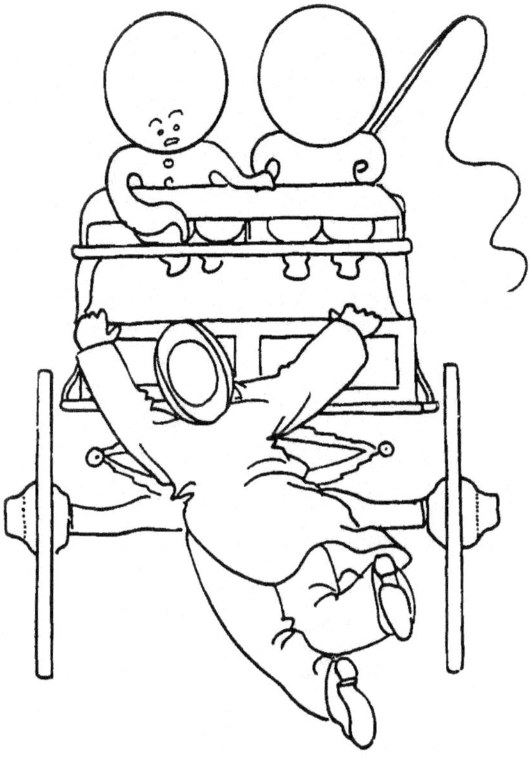

STEALING RIDES

I THOUGHT I saw a little Goop
   Who hung behind a cart;
I looked again. He'd fallen off!
   It gave me *such* a start!
"If he were killed, some day," I said,
   "'T would break his mother's heart!"

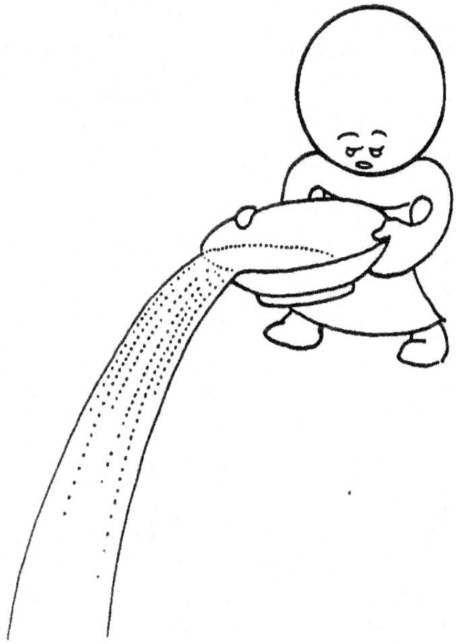

UNTIDY GOOPS

I THINK you are a Goop, because
You never shut your bureau drawers,
   You do not close the door!
You leave your water in the bowl,
You put your peelings in the coal!
   I've told you *that* before!

A GOOP PARTY

"Please come to my party!" said Jenny to Prue;
"I'm going to have Willy, and Nelly, and you;
I'm going to have candy and cake and ice-cream,
We'll play *Hunt-the-Slipper*, we'll laugh and we'll scream.
We'll dress up in caps, we'll have stories and tricks,
And you won't have to go till a quarter past six!"
But alas! When she mentioned her party, at tea,
Her mother said, "No! It can't possibly be!"
So Jane had to go and explain to her friends,
And that is how many a Goop party ends!
Just speak to your mother *before* you invite,
And then it's more likely to happen all right!

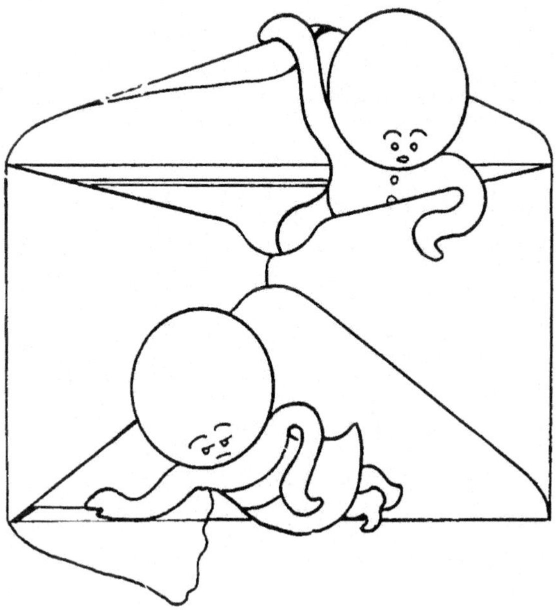

INQUISITIVENESS

I gave a letter to a Goop
  To take to Mrs. Bird;
And what d' you think he went and did?
  He read it, every word!
Now, isn't that the rudest thing
  That you have ever heard?

Why, he would peep through keyholes,
  And listen at the door!
And open parcels, just to see
  What came from every store!

Now, have you ever *ever* heard
Of such a Goop before?

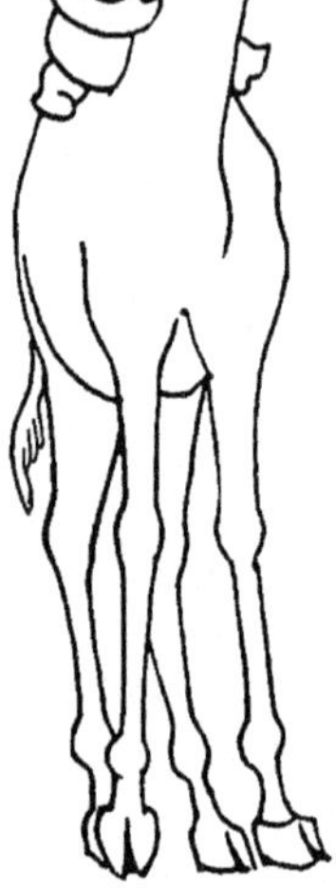

DON'T BE GOOD

Just because you want to go
To the circus, or the show;
But, when all your fun is o'er,
Be as good as you were before!

DON'T BE BAD

Just as long as you dare to be,
Because your mother does n't see.
Do not wait for her to scold,
But be just as good as gold!

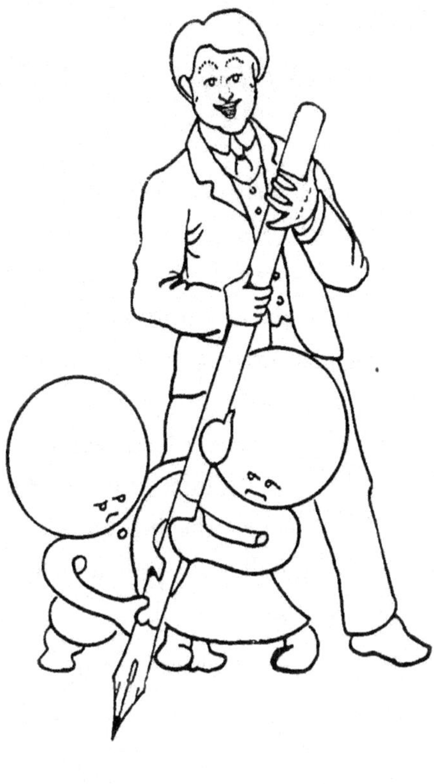

WRITE RIGHT!

If you were writing with your nose,
You 'd *have* to curl up, I suppose,
And lay your head upon your hand;
But now, I cannot understand,
For you are writing with your pen!
So sit erect, and smile again!
You need not scowl because you write,
Nor hold your fingers *quite* so tight!
And if you gnaw the holder so,
They 'll take you for
a Goop, you know!

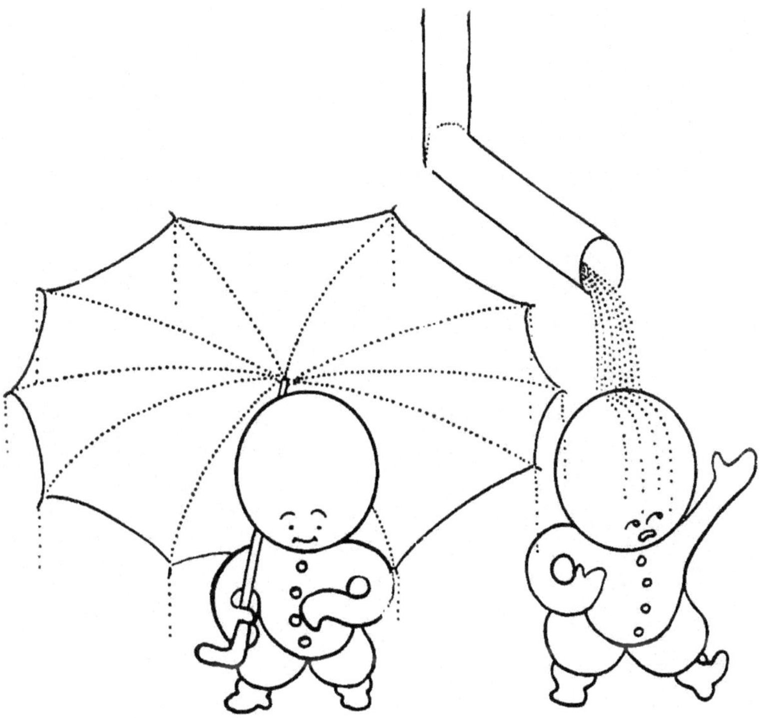

WET FEET

Down the street together,
In the rainy weather,
Went a pair of little boys along;
One of them went straying
In the gutters playing,
Doing all his mother said was wrong;

One of them went dashing
Into puddles splashing,
Under dripping eaves that soaked him through;
One of them avoided
All the other boy did,
Dodging all the slimy, slushy goo.

One of them grew chilly;
Said he felt so ill he
Knew he 'd caught a cold, and coughed a lot!
The other was so warm he
Said he *liked* it stormy!
Which of them was Goop, and which was not?

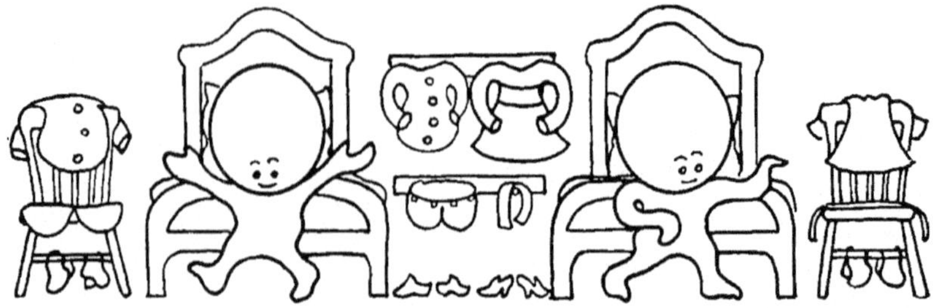

DRESS QUICKLY!

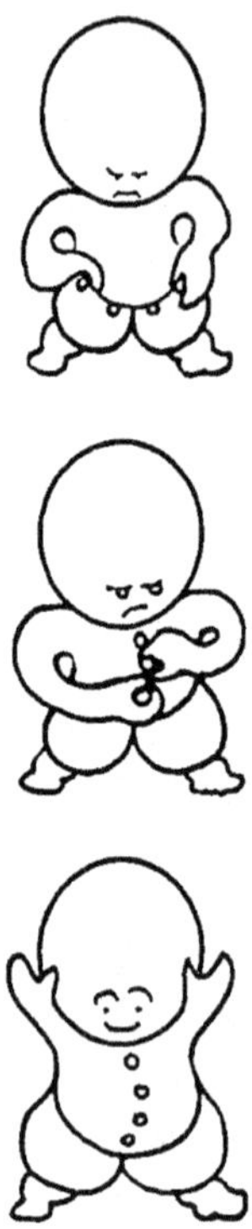

ALL your life you 'll have to dress,
Every single day (unless
You should happen to be sick),
Why not learn to do it quick?
Hang your clothes the proper way,
So you'll find them fresh next day;
Treat them with a little care,
Fold them neatly on a chair;
So, without a bit of worry,
You can dress in quite a hurry.
Think of the slovenly Goops, before
You strew your clothing on the floor!

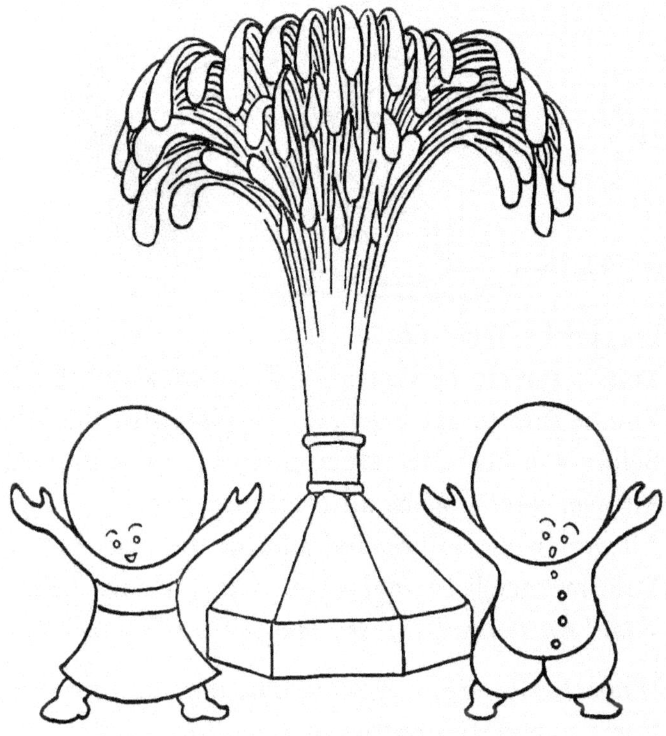

INK, ink! What do you think!
You 're sure to be stained, if you play with the ink!
You 're sure to get black, if you play with the ink-well,
Before you begin it, just stop once, and think well!
All over your fingers, all over your face,
All over your clothes, and all over the place!
Your mother'll be angry, your father'll say, "*There!*
I said not to touch it; you said you'd take care!"

When Goops are so mischievous, they have to drink
Forty-four dozen bottles of raven black ink!

THE REASON WHY

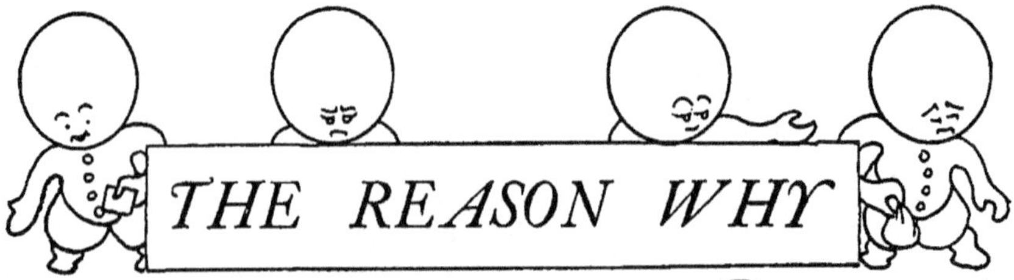

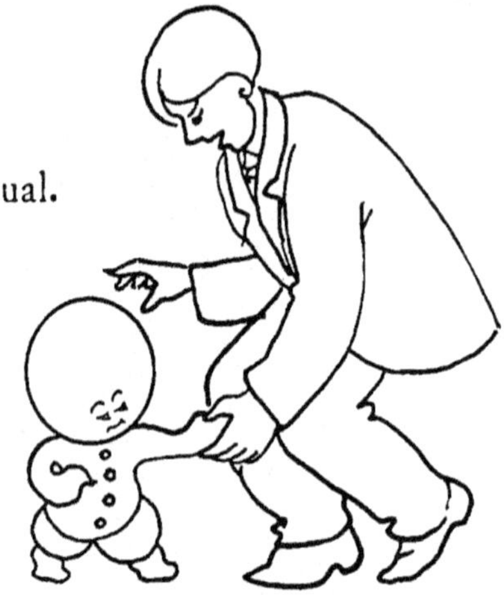

Everybody liked Ezekiel.
Why?
You could scarcely find his equal.
Why?
If he made a mistake,
He said he was wrong;
If he went on an errand,
He was n't gone long;
He never would bully,
Although he was strong!

Everybody hated Mello.
Why?
He was such a surly fellow.
Why?
If you asked him for candy,
He 'd hide his away;
He never would play
What the rest wished to play;
He would say *horrid* words
That he ought n't to say!

IN GOOP ATTIRE

I'LL make you a dress of a towel,
And trim it all over with soap,
With a sponge for a hat
And a wet one, at that!
And *then* you 'll be happy, I hope!
You may act like a Goop, if you please,
In garments constructed like these!

But now, while you 're dressed up so neatly,
Don't wipe off your hands on your frock!
The smooching that lingers
When you wipe off your fingers,
Will give your dear mother a shock!
The result
will be
even more
shocking,
If you wipe off your
shoes on your
stocking!

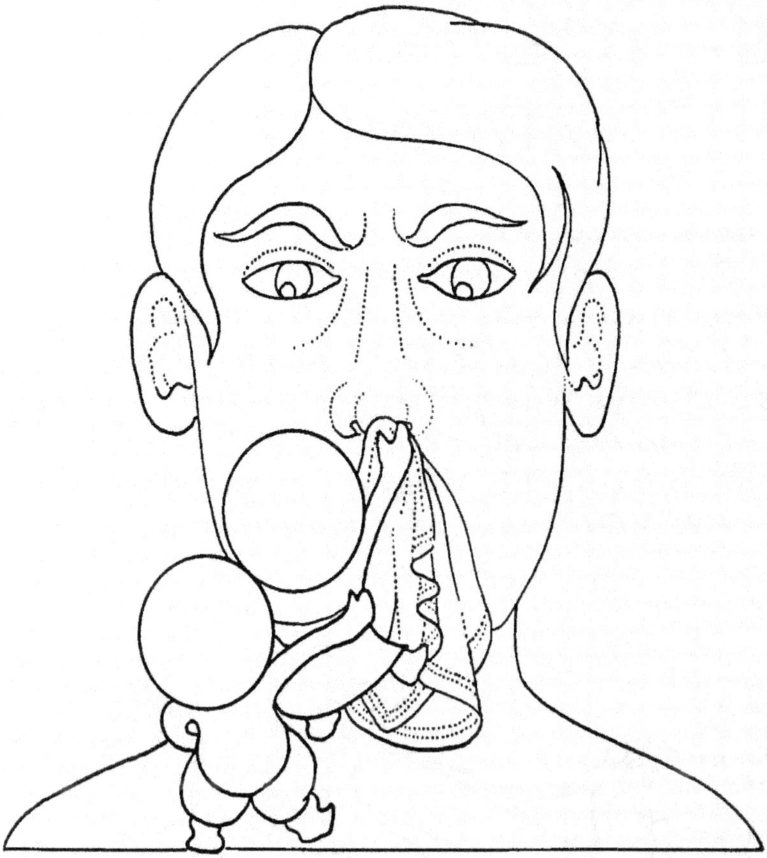

IMPOSSIBLE!

THERE once was a Goop (*it is hard to believe*
Such unpleasant behavior of you!)
Who always was wiping his nose on his sleeve;
I hope that this Goop was n't you!
He always was spitting (for fun, I suppose),
I could n't believe it of you!
And putting his fingers up into his nose;
I KNOW that this Goop was n't you!

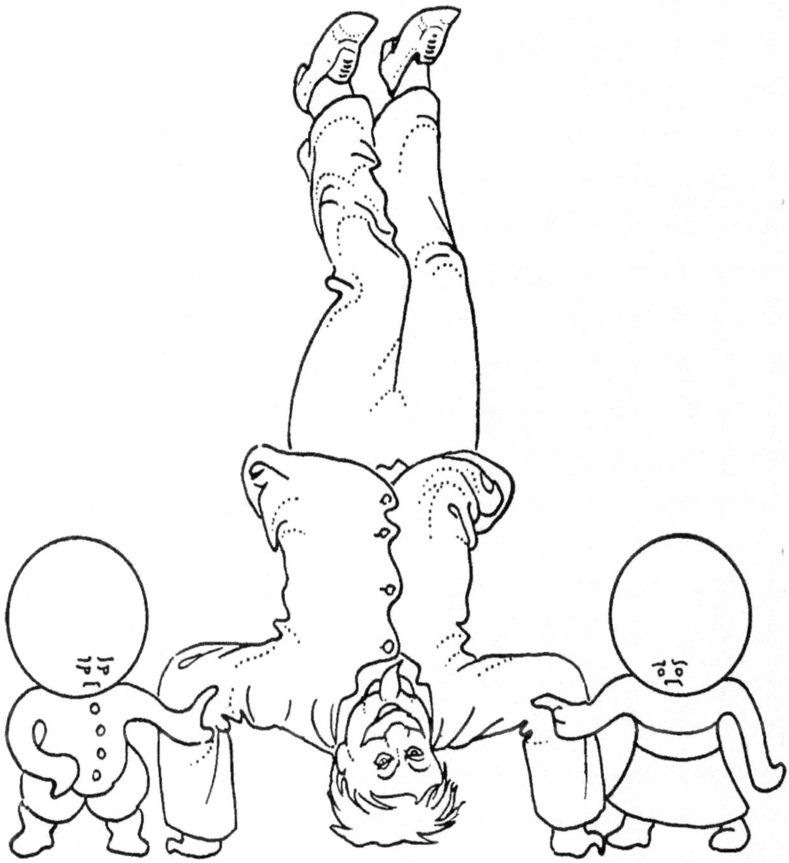

A PUZZLE

THERE are about a thousand things
  I 'm not allowed to do ;
Most everything I 'm fondest of
  I 'm told is wrong — are you ?

They say, " *Please don't do that, my child!* "
  They say, " *You must n't, dear !* "
I hope sometime I 'll learn what 's right,
  For now it seems so queer !

19
03

CPSIA information can be obtained
at www.ICGtesting.com
Printed in the USA
LVOW05s0833250817
546314LV00021B/1535/P

9 781290 551571